Mastering Emotional Intelligence: Enhancing Relationships and Self-Mastery

Christoffer Smestad

Published by Christoffer Smestad, 2023.

While every precaution has been taken in the preparation of this book, the publisher assumes no responsibility for errors or omissions, or for damages resulting from the use of the information contained herein.

MASTERING EMOTIONAL INTELLIGENCE: ENHANCING RELATIONSHIPS AND SELF-MASTERY

First edition. July 17, 2023.

Copyright © 2023 Christoffer Smestad.

ISBN: 979-8215739273

Written by Christoffer Smestad.

Table of Contents

Chapter 1: The Foundations of Emotional Intelligence

Understanding emotional intelligence and its importance in personal and professional life

In this chapter, we will explore the concept of emotional intelligence (EI) and its significant role in shaping our personal and professional lives. Emotional intelligence refers to our ability to recognize, understand, and manage our own emotions, as well as effectively navigate and respond to the emotions of others.

Emotional intelligence comprises five key components that work together to form a comprehensive understanding of our emotional capabilities:

1. Self-awareness: The ability to recognize and understand our own emotions, strengths, weaknesses, and values. It involves being aware of our thoughts, feelings, and reactions in various situations.
2. Self-regulation: The capacity to effectively manage and control our emotions, impulses, and behaviors. It encompasses skills such as emotional control, adaptability, and resilience in the face of challenges.
3. Motivation: The drive and determination to set and achieve meaningful goals. Motivation fuels our passion, perseverance, and resilience, enabling us to overcome obstacles and stay focused on our aspirations.
4. Empathy: The ability to understand and share the feelings of others. Empathy involves putting ourselves in someone else's shoes, being attuned to their emotions, and responding with compassion and understanding.

5. Social skills: The aptitude to navigate social interactions, build relationships, and communicate effectively. Social skills encompass active listening, conflict resolution, teamwork, and the ability to influence and inspire others.

Understanding and developing emotional intelligence is crucial because it brings numerous benefits to our personal and professional lives. By honing our emotional intelligence, we improve our relationships, communication skills, and conflict resolution abilities. It allows us to have a deeper understanding of ourselves and others, fostering empathy and creating stronger connections. Emotional intelligence also enhances our decision-making abilities, leadership skills, and overall well-being.

As we embark on this exploration of emotional intelligence, we will delve deeper into each component, understanding its significance and discovering practical techniques to enhance our emotional intelligence. Together, we will uncover the power of emotional intelligence in shaping our lives for the better.

Stay tuned for an enlightening journey into the world of emotional intelligence.

Practical techniques for improving self-awareness

In this section, we will explore practical techniques that can help enhance self-awareness, a critical component of emotional intelligence. Self-awareness allows us to recognize and understand our own emotions, thoughts, and behavioral patterns. By developing a deeper understanding of ourselves, we can make conscious choices and better navigate our emotions and interactions with others.

1. Mindfulness practice: Engaging in mindfulness exercises can heighten self-awareness. Set aside dedicated time each day to focus on the present moment without judgment. Pay attention

to your thoughts, emotions, and physical sensations, observing them without attachment. Through regular mindfulness practice, you can become more aware of your internal experiences and gain insights into your patterns of thinking and reacting.

2. Journaling: Keeping a journal can be a valuable tool for self-reflection and self-awareness. Set aside time to write down your thoughts, feelings, and experiences. Reflect on your emotions, triggers, and patterns that arise throughout the day. Journaling provides a safe space for exploration and self-expression, helping you gain clarity and insights into your inner world.

3. Seeking feedback: Actively seek feedback from trusted individuals in your life, such as friends, family, or mentors. Their perspectives can provide valuable insights into how others perceive you and your behavior. Be open to constructive criticism and use it as an opportunity for growth and self-improvement.

4. Reflective questioning: Engage in reflective questioning to deepen your self-awareness. Ask yourself thought-provoking questions, such as "What emotions am I experiencing right now?" or "How does this situation align with my values?" Reflect on your responses and explore the underlying motivations, beliefs, and emotions that drive your thoughts and actions.

5. Emotional check-ins: Throughout the day, take brief pauses to check in with your emotions. Notice how you are feeling in different situations and environments. This practice helps you develop a better understanding of your emotional states, allowing you to respond consciously rather than react impulsively.

6. Feedback from experiences: Reflect on your experiences, both positive and negative, to gain insights about yourself. Consider

how you reacted in various situations and the impact of your actions on yourself and others. Learn from these experiences and use them as opportunities for self-awareness and personal growth.

By incorporating these practical techniques into your daily life, you can cultivate self-awareness and deepen your understanding of your own emotions, thoughts, and behaviors. Developing self-awareness lays the foundation for enhancing emotional intelligence and fosters personal growth and meaningful connections with others.

Strategies for developing self-regulation skills

In this section, we will explore strategies and techniques that can help you develop self-regulation skills, an essential component of emotional intelligence. Self-regulation involves effectively managing and controlling your emotions, impulses, and behaviors. By developing self-regulation skills, you can respond to situations with composure, adaptability, and emotional balance.

1. Recognize and label emotions: Practice identifying and labeling your emotions as they arise. Take a moment to pause and reflect on what you are feeling, giving each emotion a name. This simple act of recognition helps create distance between you and your emotions, allowing you to respond thoughtfully rather than react impulsively.
2. Breath awareness and relaxation techniques: Cultivate relaxation techniques such as deep breathing exercises, progressive muscle relaxation, or mindfulness meditation. These practices help calm the nervous system, reduce stress, and promote emotional balance. When faced with challenging situations, take a few deep breaths to center yourself and regain composure.

3. Develop emotional resilience: Emotional resilience allows you to bounce back from setbacks and adversity. Cultivate resilience by reframing challenges as opportunities for growth, practicing positive self-talk, and seeking support from others when needed. Embrace a growth mindset that views obstacles as temporary setbacks rather than permanent barriers.

4. Create an emotional regulation toolkit: Build a toolkit of strategies that help you regulate your emotions in different situations. This toolkit may include activities such as physical exercise, engaging in hobbies or creative outlets, listening to calming music, or practicing mindfulness. Experiment with various techniques and identify what works best for you in managing your emotions.

5. Practice self-care: Prioritize self-care activities that support your overall well-being. Take care of your physical health by maintaining a balanced diet, getting enough sleep, and engaging in regular exercise. Additionally, engage in activities that bring you joy and relaxation, such as spending time in nature, practicing self-reflection, or enjoying hobbies that recharge you.

6. Pause before responding: Develop the habit of pausing before responding in challenging situations. When faced with a triggering event or conflict, take a moment to collect your thoughts and consider the most appropriate response. This pause allows you to respond consciously rather than reacting impulsively, leading to more effective communication and problem-solving.

7. Set realistic goals: Establish realistic goals for yourself, both short-term and long-term. Break down larger goals into smaller, achievable steps. This approach helps you stay motivated, maintain focus, and avoid feeling overwhelmed, ultimately contributing to better self-regulation.

By implementing these strategies and techniques, you can strengthen your self-regulation skills and enhance your emotional intelligence. Developing the ability to manage your emotions effectively allows you to navigate challenges, maintain composure, and build healthier relationships. With practice and persistence, self-regulation becomes a valuable tool for personal growth and overall well-being.

Cultivating motivation and goal-setting

In this section, we will explore strategies for cultivating motivation and setting meaningful goals, two crucial aspects of emotional intelligence. Motivation is the driving force behind our actions and behaviors, while goal-setting provides a clear direction for our efforts. By understanding how to cultivate motivation and set effective goals, you can enhance your emotional intelligence and strive towards personal and professional fulfillment.

1. Identify intrinsic motivators: Reflect on the values, passions, and interests that inspire and energize you from within. These intrinsic motivators serve as powerful sources of motivation. Align your goals and actions with these motivators to fuel your drive and enthusiasm.
2. Clarify your vision and purpose: Take time to reflect on your long-term vision and purpose in life. What do you want to achieve? What legacy do you want to leave behind? Clarifying your vision helps you set meaningful goals that resonate with your core values and aspirations.
3. Set SMART goals: Use the SMART goal-setting framework to create clear and achievable objectives. SMART stands for Specific, Measurable, Attainable, Relevant, and Time-bound. Setting SMART goals provides structure and focus, ensuring that your efforts are directed towards tangible outcomes.
4. Break goals into smaller milestones: Break down larger goals

into smaller, manageable milestones. This approach allows you to track progress, celebrate achievements along the way, and maintain motivation. Each milestone serves as a stepping stone towards your larger goal.

5. Create an action plan: Develop a detailed action plan that outlines the specific steps and resources needed to accomplish your goals. Break down each milestone into actionable tasks and set deadlines. This plan provides a roadmap for your journey and keeps you accountable.

6. Visualize success: Practice visualization techniques to imagine yourself achieving your goals. Visualize the desired outcomes, vividly imagining how it feels to accomplish what you set out to achieve. This technique enhances motivation and creates a positive mindset.

7. Find accountability and support: Share your goals with trusted friends, family, or mentors who can provide accountability and support. Regularly update them on your progress and seek their encouragement and guidance. Having a support system increases motivation and helps you stay on track.

8. Embrace growth mindset: Adopt a growth mindset that believes in the power of learning, effort, and resilience. Embrace challenges as opportunities for growth, view setbacks as valuable learning experiences, and maintain a belief in your ability to improve and succeed.

9. Celebrate achievements: Acknowledge and celebrate your accomplishments along the way, no matter how small. Celebrating milestones reinforces positive habits, boosts motivation, and provides a sense of fulfillment and encouragement for continued progress.

By cultivating motivation and setting meaningful goals, you empower yourself to pursue personal and professional growth. With a clear vision, well-defined goals, and a motivated mindset, you can navigate obstacles, overcome setbacks, and experience the satisfaction of progress and achievement. Cultivating motivation and effective goal-setting fuels your journey toward emotional intelligence and a purpose-driven life.

Chapter 2: Developing Self-Awareness

Reflecting on your thoughts, emotions, and behavioral patterns

In this chapter, we will delve into the importance of self-awareness and explore techniques to develop a deeper understanding of your thoughts, emotions, and behavioral patterns. Self-awareness is the foundation of emotional intelligence, as it allows you to recognize and comprehend your own inner world. By gaining insight into your thoughts, emotions, and behavioral tendencies, you can make conscious choices and cultivate personal growth.

1. Mindfulness meditation: Engage in mindfulness meditation to bring your attention to the present moment and develop a non-judgmental awareness of your thoughts and emotions. Set aside a few minutes each day to practice mindfulness, focusing on your breath, bodily sensations, and the thoughts passing through your mind. This practice cultivates a heightened sense of self-awareness.

2. Daily journaling: Dedicate time to write in a journal every day, allowing yourself to freely express your thoughts and emotions. Use this as an opportunity to reflect on your experiences, analyze recurring patterns, and gain insights into your emotional states. Writing in a journal promotes self-reflection and helps uncover underlying thoughts and beliefs.

3. Emotional check-ins: Throughout the day, pause and check in with yourself. Take a moment to identify and label your emotions. Ask yourself how you are feeling and why. This simple practice increases your awareness of your emotional states and provides an opportunity to respond consciously to your emotions.

4. Seek feedback from others: Request feedback from trusted

individuals in your life, such as friends, family, or mentors. Their perspectives can offer valuable insights into your behaviors and how others perceive you. Be open to constructive criticism and use it as an opportunity for self-reflection and personal growth.

5. Engage in self-reflection exercises: Set aside dedicated time for self-reflection exercises that encourage introspection and self-awareness. Ask yourself thought-provoking questions about your values, aspirations, and the impact of your actions on yourself and others. Reflect on your strengths, weaknesses, and areas for improvement.

6. Practice active listening: Develop the skill of active listening in your interactions with others. Pay attention not only to what is being said, but also to non-verbal cues and the underlying emotions of the speaker. Actively listening promotes empathy and allows you to better understand your own reactions and triggers.

7. Use self-assessment tools: Utilize self-assessment tools, such as personality assessments or emotional intelligence questionnaires, to gain insights into your personality traits, strengths, and areas of growth. These tools can provide valuable starting points for self-reflection and self-awareness.

By incorporating these techniques into your daily life, you can deepen your self-awareness and gain a better understanding of your thoughts, emotions, and behavioral patterns. Developing self-awareness allows you to make conscious choices aligned with your values, manage your emotions effectively, and enhance your overall emotional intelligence. Embrace the journey of self-discovery and self-reflection as you cultivate self-awareness and unlock new levels of personal growth.

Exploring your strengths, weaknesses, and areas for growth

In this section, we will focus on exploring your strengths, weaknesses, and areas for growth as part of developing self-awareness. Understanding your unique qualities and areas of improvement allows you to make conscious decisions and pursue personal growth effectively.

1. Identify your strengths: Take time to reflect on your personal strengths and the qualities that come naturally to you. Consider the skills, talents, and characteristics that you excel in and bring value to your life and those around you. Acknowledging your strengths enhances self-confidence and provides a foundation for personal growth.

2. Reflect on your weaknesses: Engage in honest self-reflection and identify areas where you may have weaknesses or areas that require improvement. Recognize that acknowledging weaknesses is not a sign of failure but an opportunity for growth. Embrace a growth mindset and view weaknesses as areas where you can invest effort and develop new skills.

3. Seek feedback from others: Ask for feedback from trusted individuals who can provide insights into your strengths, weaknesses, and blind spots. Listen attentively to their observations and perspectives, and consider how they align with your self-perception. Integrating feedback from others can help you gain a more comprehensive understanding of yourself.

4. Set goals for personal development: Based on your self-reflection, identify specific goals for personal development. Focus on areas where you would like to improve or acquire new skills. Set realistic and actionable goals that align with your values and long-term aspirations. Breaking these goals down into smaller steps can make them more manageable and achievable.

5. Embrace a growth mindset: Adopt a growth mindset, which

believes that abilities and intelligence can be developed through dedication and effort. Embrace challenges as opportunities for growth and view setbacks as learning experiences. Cultivate resilience and persistence in the face of obstacles, knowing that they are essential components of the growth process.

6. Continuous learning and self-improvement: Commit to lifelong learning and self-improvement. Engage in activities that expand your knowledge, skills, and perspectives. Seek out new experiences, take courses or workshops, read books on topics of interest, and actively pursue personal and professional development opportunities.

7. Celebrate progress and achievements: Recognize and celebrate your progress and achievements along the way. Acknowledge the steps you have taken towards personal growth and the positive changes you have made. Celebrating milestones reinforces positive habits, boosts motivation, and encourages continued self-improvement.

By exploring your strengths, weaknesses, and areas for growth, you gain a deeper understanding of yourself and can make intentional choices to enhance your personal and professional life. Embrace your strengths, address your weaknesses, set goals for personal development, and cultivate a growth mindset. Remember that personal growth is a continuous journey, and each step you take brings you closer to realizing your fullest potential.

Building self-acceptance and embracing your authentic self

In this section, we will focus on building self-acceptance and embracing your authentic self as essential components of self-awareness. Developing self-acceptance allows you to embrace your strengths and weaknesses, cultivate a positive self-image, and live authentically.

1. Practice self-compassion: Treat yourself with kindness, understanding, and compassion. Acknowledge that everyone has strengths and weaknesses, and it's okay to make mistakes or experience setbacks. Offer yourself the same empathy and support you would extend to a close friend or loved one.
2. Challenge self-judgment: Notice and challenge any self-judgment or self-criticism that arises within you. Replace negative self-talk with positive affirmations and supportive statements. Focus on your progress and achievements rather than dwelling on perceived shortcomings.
3. Embrace your uniqueness: Celebrate your individuality and the qualities that make you unique. Recognize that your strengths, talents, and perspectives contribute to the richness of your character. Embrace your authentic self and honor your true nature.
4. Cultivate self-awareness without judgment: Foster a non-judgmental awareness of your thoughts, emotions, and actions. Practice observing yourself without attaching labels or evaluations. Allow yourself to experience your emotions fully without judgment, understanding that they are a natural part of being human.
5. Seek alignment with values: Reflect on your core values and ensure that your actions and decisions align with them. Living in accordance with your values enhances self-acceptance and promotes authenticity. When you honor your values, you create a sense of integrity and congruence within yourself.
6. Surround yourself with support: Build a network of supportive individuals who accept and appreciate you for who you are. Surrounding yourself with people who celebrate your uniqueness and encourage your personal growth fosters a sense of belonging and acceptance.
7. Practice authenticity in communication: Be genuine and

authentic in your interactions with others. Express your thoughts, emotions, and opinions honestly and respectfully. Embracing authenticity fosters deeper connections and allows others to know and understand the real you.

8. Engage in self-care: Prioritize self-care practices that nurture your physical, mental, and emotional well-being. Engaging in activities that bring you joy, relaxation, and fulfillment promotes self-acceptance and self-connection.

By building self-acceptance and embracing your authentic self, you cultivate a deep sense of self-awareness and create a foundation for personal growth and well-being. Remember that your uniqueness is your strength, and living authentically allows you to lead a fulfilling and purposeful life. Embrace self-compassion, challenge self-judgment, and surround yourself with support as you embark on this journey of self-acceptance and self-discovery.

Exploring the impact of beliefs and mindset on self-awareness

In this section, we will explore the impact of beliefs and mindset on self-awareness. Our beliefs shape our perception of ourselves, others, and the world around us. Understanding the power of our beliefs and cultivating a growth mindset can enhance self-awareness and foster personal growth.

1. Examine limiting beliefs: Identify and examine any limiting beliefs you may hold about yourself. These beliefs can be self-imposed limitations that hinder your self-awareness and personal growth. Challenge these beliefs by questioning their validity and replacing them with empowering and supportive beliefs.

2. Cultivate a growth mindset: Embrace a growth mindset, which views challenges as opportunities for learning and growth.

Believe that your abilities and intelligence can be developed through effort, practice, and perseverance. Adopting a growth mindset allows you to embrace feedback, see failures as stepping stones to success, and continually seek opportunities for self-improvement.

3. Practice reframing: Reframing involves consciously shifting your perspective on challenging situations. Instead of seeing them as obstacles, reframe them as opportunities for growth and learning. This shift in mindset allows you to approach challenges with curiosity and resilience, enhancing self-awareness and personal development.

4. Question assumptions: Challenge the assumptions you make about yourself and others. Often, our beliefs and assumptions are based on limited information or past experiences. Engage in critical thinking and question the validity of these assumptions. Seek evidence that supports or challenges your beliefs to gain a more accurate understanding of yourself and the world.

5. Embrace self-reflection: Regularly engage in self-reflection to examine your thoughts, emotions, and behaviors. This introspective practice allows you to identify patterns, uncover underlying beliefs, and gain clarity on how they influence your self-awareness. Self-reflection fosters a deeper understanding of yourself and provides opportunities for personal growth.

6. Seek diverse perspectives: Seek out diverse perspectives and engage in conversations with individuals who have different viewpoints and life experiences. This exposure to varied perspectives challenges your beliefs, expands your understanding of yourself and others, and enhances self-awareness.

7. Embrace lifelong learning: Cultivate a mindset of lifelong learning and continuous growth. Approach each experience as

an opportunity to gain new knowledge, insights, and perspectives. Embracing a learning mindset broadens your horizons, enhances self-awareness, and keeps you open to new possibilities.

By exploring the impact of beliefs and mindset on self-awareness, you can challenge limiting beliefs, adopt a growth mindset, and develop a more accurate understanding of yourself and the world. Cultivating a mindset of curiosity, open-mindedness, and continuous learning enables you to expand your self-awareness and embrace personal growth opportunities. Embrace the power of beliefs and mindset as catalysts for self-awareness and self-transformation.

Chapter 3: Cultivating Empathy and Compassion

Understanding the importance of empathy in building meaningful connections

In this chapter, we will explore the significance of empathy in cultivating meaningful connections with others. Empathy is the ability to understand and share the feelings of others, stepping into their shoes and seeing the world from their perspective. By developing empathy, you can foster deeper connections, enhance communication, and promote understanding and compassion in your relationships.

1. Empathy as a bridge: Recognize empathy as a bridge that connects us to others on an emotional level. By understanding and acknowledging the emotions of others, we can establish rapport, build trust, and create a supportive environment for open communication.
2. Active listening: Practice active listening, which involves giving your full attention to the speaker, suspending judgment, and truly seeking to understand their perspective. Maintain eye contact, use non-verbal cues to show engagement, and reflect back their thoughts and feelings to demonstrate that you are actively present and empathetically attuned.
3. Perspective-taking: Cultivate the ability to step into the shoes of others and see the world through their eyes. Imagine their experiences, thoughts, and emotions without judgment. This exercise broadens your understanding, breaks down barriers, and enhances empathy.
4. Cultivate curiosity and open-mindedness: Approach conversations and interactions with curiosity and an open mind. Seek to understand different viewpoints and

experiences, even if they differ from your own. Curiosity fosters empathy by encouraging a genuine interest in others and a willingness to learn from their perspectives.

5. Practice empathy in difficult situations: Challenge yourself to extend empathy even in challenging or conflict-ridden situations. By seeking to understand the underlying emotions and needs of others, you can promote empathy and compassion even in moments of tension.

6. Validate emotions: Validate the emotions of others by acknowledging and accepting them without judgment. Letting others know that their emotions are valid and understood creates a safe and supportive environment for emotional expression and fosters deeper connections.

7. Practice self-empathy: Develop empathy towards yourself as well. Be kind and compassionate towards your own emotions and experiences. Recognize that self-compassion and self-care are essential in nurturing empathy towards others.

8. Seek diverse perspectives: Actively seek out diverse perspectives and experiences. Engage in conversations and activities that expose you to different cultures, backgrounds, and viewpoints. This broadens your understanding of the human experience and enhances your empathetic capacity.

By understanding the importance of empathy and incorporating empathetic practices into your interactions, you can foster meaningful connections and create a more compassionate and understanding world. Embracing empathy allows you to build bridges of understanding, deepen relationships, and contribute to a more empathetic and harmonious society.

Developing effective communication skills for empathetic interactions

In this section, we will focus on developing effective communication skills that support empathetic interactions. Effective communication plays a vital role in expressing empathy, understanding others, and building strong relationships. By honing your communication skills, you can foster empathetic connections and promote understanding and collaboration.

1. Active listening: Engage in active listening to demonstrate empathy and understanding. Give your full attention to the speaker, maintain eye contact, and avoid interrupting. Show genuine interest in their words, and reflect back their thoughts and feelings to convey that you are attentively listening and understanding their perspective.

2. Verbal and non-verbal cues: Pay attention to both verbal and non-verbal cues during conversations. Non-verbal cues such as facial expressions, body language, and tone of voice can provide valuable insights into the emotions and intentions behind the words. Align your own non-verbal cues with empathy, such as nodding, maintaining an open posture, and using a warm and compassionate tone.

3. Empathetic language: Use empathetic language that validates and acknowledges the emotions of others. Phrases such as "I understand how you feel," "That must be challenging," or "I'm here for you" convey empathy and create a safe space for emotional expression. Be mindful of your tone and choice of words, ensuring they reflect compassion and understanding.

4. Ask open-ended questions: Encourage deeper conversations and understanding by asking open-ended questions. These questions invite the speaker to share more about their thoughts, feelings, and experiences. Open-ended questions promote empathy by demonstrating a genuine interest in the other person's perspective and fostering a dialogue that goes

beyond surface-level interactions.

5. Practice empathy through reflection: Reflect back the thoughts and emotions of the speaker to show that you understand and empathize with their experience. Paraphrase their words and summarize their feelings to demonstrate active listening and empathy. This reflection validates their emotions and deepens the connection between both parties.

6. Emotional intelligence in difficult conversations: Apply emotional intelligence skills during challenging or sensitive conversations. Stay calm and composed, regulate your emotions, and choose your words carefully. Be mindful of the impact of your words on others and aim for a collaborative and understanding approach.

7. Seek clarification: If there is any ambiguity or misunderstanding, seek clarification to ensure accurate comprehension. Ask follow-up questions to gain clarity and avoid making assumptions. Clarifying your understanding demonstrates respect, active engagement, and a commitment to empathetic communication.

8. Practice empathy in digital communication: Extend empathy to digital communication channels, such as email, text messages, or online conversations. Be mindful of the potential for misinterpretation and take extra care in conveying your empathy through written words. Use emoticons, thoughtful language, and considerate tone to express empathy effectively.

By developing effective communication skills grounded in empathy, you can create meaningful connections, foster understanding, and build strong relationships. Enhancing your communication abilities allows you to express empathy genuinely, foster collaboration, and contribute to a more empathetic and compassionate society. Embrace these communication practices and witness the transformative power of empathetic interactions.

Cultivating empathy through perspective-taking and active curiosity

In this section, we will explore the practices of perspective-taking and active curiosity as powerful tools for cultivating empathy. Perspective-taking involves stepping into someone else's shoes and seeing the world from their viewpoint, while active curiosity involves a genuine interest in understanding others. By developing these skills, you can deepen your empathy and foster stronger connections with those around you.

1. Practice perspective-taking: Make a conscious effort to understand others' perspectives, even if they differ from your own. Imagine how they might feel, think, and perceive a situation based on their unique experiences and background. This exercise helps you broaden your understanding, challenge assumptions, and foster empathy.

2. Suspend judgment: When engaging with others, strive to suspend judgment and approach their experiences and viewpoints with an open mind. Recognize that everyone has a unique story and set of circumstances that shape their perspective. Avoid jumping to conclusions or making assumptions, and instead, seek to understand their perspective before forming opinions.

3. Active curiosity: Cultivate an active curiosity about others' experiences, thoughts, and emotions. Ask open-ended questions that invite them to share more about their perspectives and stories. Show genuine interest in learning from them and understanding their unique viewpoints. Curiosity promotes empathy by demonstrating a willingness to listen and learn from others.

4. Empathetic imagination: Use your imagination to put yourself in the shoes of others. Visualize their experiences, emotions, and challenges. Imagine how you would feel if you were in their situation. This empathetic imagination helps bridge the gap between different perspectives and enhances understanding and compassion.

5. Seek diverse perspectives: Actively seek out diverse perspectives and expose yourself to different cultures, backgrounds, and viewpoints. Engage in conversations and activities that bring you in contact with people from various walks of life. The more you expose yourself to diverse perspectives, the more you broaden your empathy and understanding of others.

6. Listen with empathy: Develop the skill of empathetic listening by being fully present and attuned to the emotions and needs of the speaker. Practice listening without interrupting or imposing your own opinions. Show empathy through your non-verbal cues, such as maintaining eye contact, nodding, and providing verbal affirmations.

7. Validate emotions and experiences: Validate the emotions and experiences of others by acknowledging their feelings and affirming their worth. Let them know that their experiences and emotions are valid, even if they differ from your own. This validation creates a safe and empathetic space for open and honest communication.

8. Cultivate cultural competence: Educate yourself about different cultures, traditions, and norms to develop cultural competence. This understanding allows you to navigate cultural differences with respect and empathy. Embrace diversity and strive to celebrate the richness that different cultures bring to our interconnected world.

By cultivating perspective-taking and active curiosity, you can deepen your empathy and understanding of others. These practices enable you to connect on a deeper level, appreciate diverse perspectives, and foster a more empathetic and inclusive society. Embrace the power of perspective-taking and active curiosity as catalysts for empathy and positive change in your relationships and communities.

Empathy in action: Practicing acts of kindness and compassion

In this section, we will explore how empathy can be put into action through acts of kindness and compassion. Practicing empathy goes beyond understanding others' emotions; it involves taking steps to make a positive impact and show genuine care for others. By actively practicing acts of kindness and compassion, you can create a ripple effect of empathy and contribute to a more compassionate world.

1. Random acts of kindness: Engage in random acts of kindness to brighten someone's day. Small gestures, such as offering a genuine compliment, holding the door for someone, or helping someone in need, can make a significant difference in their lives. These acts demonstrate empathy and show that you care about the well-being of others.

2. Volunteer and support causes: Get involved in volunteering or supporting causes that align with your values and ignite your passion. Offer your time, skills, or resources to organizations or initiatives that help those in need. By actively contributing to causes that promote well-being and equality, you exemplify empathy in action.

3. Practice active compassion: Cultivate an active compassion that drives you to alleviate the suffering of others. Listen attentively to their challenges, offer support and encouragement, and extend a helping hand. Show genuine care and empathy by being present for others during difficult times.

4. Practice empathy in conflict resolution: When conflicts arise, approach them with empathy and a desire to understand all perspectives involved. Listen actively to each person's concerns, acknowledge their emotions, and work towards finding mutually beneficial resolutions. Empathetic conflict resolution fosters understanding, reconciliation, and stronger relationships.

5. Cultivate empathy in your everyday interactions: Infuse empathy into your everyday interactions with family, friends, colleagues, and strangers. Practice active listening, express genuine interest in others' experiences, and offer support and understanding. Small acts of empathy, such as being a compassionate listener or showing empathy during someone's struggle, can have a profound impact.

6. Practice self-compassion: Extend empathy and kindness to yourself through self-compassion practices. Treat yourself with the same understanding and care you would offer to others. Be gentle with your own mistakes, acknowledge your emotions, and prioritize self-care. Practicing self-compassion allows you to replenish your own empathy reserves and be more present for others.

7. Foster a culture of empathy: Be an advocate for empathy in your community and encourage others to practice kindness and compassion. Engage in conversations that promote empathy, share inspiring stories, and lead by example. By fostering a culture of empathy, you create an environment where compassion thrives and positive change can occur.

8. Reflect on the impact of your actions: Take time to reflect on the impact of your acts of kindness and compassion. Notice how they affect others and the ripple effect they create. Recognize that even small acts of empathy can have far-reaching consequences, inspiring others to practice empathy as

well.

By putting empathy into action through acts of kindness and compassion, you contribute to a more empathetic and caring world. Embrace opportunities to extend empathy in your interactions, support causes that promote well-being, and practice self-compassion. Each act of kindness and compassion enhances the collective empathy of our society and brings us closer to creating a more harmonious and compassionate world.

Chapter 4: Cultivating Resilience and Emotional Well-being

Understanding resilience and its role in emotional well-being

In this chapter, we will explore the concept of resilience and its crucial role in cultivating emotional well-being. Resilience refers to the ability to adapt, bounce back, and thrive in the face of adversity, challenges, and stress. By understanding resilience and developing strategies to enhance it, you can nurture your emotional well-being and navigate life's ups and downs with greater strength and resilience.

1. Definition of resilience: Gain a clear understanding of what resilience means. Recognize that resilience is not the absence of difficulties but rather the ability to effectively cope, adapt, and recover from them. Embrace the idea that resilience is a skill that can be developed and strengthened through practice.

2. Building a support system: Foster a strong support system by nurturing relationships with trusted friends, family members, or mentors. Surround yourself with individuals who uplift and support you during challenging times. Having a reliable support network provides emotional support, encouragement, and a sense of belonging.

3. Developing positive coping strategies: Explore and develop positive coping strategies that help you manage stress, adversity, and emotional challenges. These strategies may include exercise, mindfulness, creative outlets, journaling, or engaging in activities that bring you joy and relaxation. Find what works best for you and integrate these practices into your daily life.

4. Cultivating a growth mindset: Embrace a growth mindset that sees setbacks as opportunities for growth and learning. Instead

of viewing obstacles as insurmountable, see them as temporary roadblocks that can be overcome. Foster a belief in your ability to learn, adapt, and develop resilience through experience.

5. Enhancing self-care practices: Prioritize self-care as a means of maintaining emotional well-being and building resilience. Engage in activities that nurture your physical, mental, and emotional health, such as getting adequate sleep, eating nutritious food, practicing self-compassion, and setting healthy boundaries. Taking care of yourself equips you to better handle challenges and build resilience.

6. Cultivating optimism and positive thinking: Foster optimism and positive thinking as a way to reframe challenges and setbacks. Focus on the possibilities and opportunities that arise from difficult situations. Practice gratitude and develop a habit of acknowledging the positive aspects of your life, even in challenging times.

7. Embracing self-reflection and growth: Engage in regular self-reflection to identify areas for personal growth and development. Use setbacks and challenges as opportunities to learn about yourself, strengthen your resilience, and build emotional well-being. Embrace a mindset of continuous growth and self-improvement.

8. Developing problem-solving skills: Enhance your problem-solving skills to effectively navigate challenges. Break down problems into manageable steps, brainstorm potential solutions, and take action towards finding resolutions. Developing strong problem-solving abilities enhances resilience by empowering you to take control and find solutions even in difficult circumstances.

By understanding resilience and incorporating strategies to cultivate it, you can nurture your emotional well-being and thrive in the face of adversity. Embrace the belief in your own resilience, build a strong support system, engage in self-care practices, and foster a growth mindset. Cultivating resilience equips you with the tools to face life's challenges, bounce back from setbacks, and lead a more emotionally balanced and fulfilling life.

Developing emotional regulation and stress management techniques

In this section, we will focus on developing emotional regulation and stress management techniques to enhance resilience and emotional well-being. Emotions play a significant role in our lives, and being able to regulate and manage them effectively contributes to overall resilience and emotional balance.

1. Emotional awareness: Cultivate emotional awareness by tuning into your emotions and recognizing their presence. Pay attention to the physical sensations, thoughts, and behaviors associated with different emotions. Developing emotional awareness allows you to better understand and respond to your emotions in a constructive manner.

2. Mindfulness practice: Engage in mindfulness practices, such as meditation or deep breathing exercises, to cultivate present-moment awareness and reduce stress. Mindfulness helps you observe your thoughts and emotions without judgment, promoting emotional regulation and reducing reactivity.

3. Stress reduction techniques: Explore various stress reduction techniques that work for you, such as physical exercise, yoga, progressive muscle relaxation, or engaging in hobbies that bring you joy and relaxation. These techniques help alleviate stress, promote relaxation, and enhance emotional well-being.

4. Cognitive reframing: Practice cognitive reframing by challenging and replacing negative or unhelpful thoughts with more positive and realistic ones. Identify cognitive distortions,

such as black-and-white thinking or catastrophizing, and reframe them to create a more balanced perspective. This practice can help regulate emotions and reduce stress.

5. Healthy coping strategies: Develop healthy coping strategies to manage stress and emotional challenges. These strategies may include seeking social support, engaging in creative outlets, journaling, practicing self-compassion, or seeking professional help when needed. Healthy coping mechanisms empower you to effectively navigate and manage difficult emotions.

6. Time management and prioritization: Improve your time management skills and prioritize tasks to reduce stress and overwhelm. Breaking tasks into smaller, manageable steps and setting realistic deadlines helps create a sense of control and reduces emotional strain.

7. Setting boundaries: Establish clear boundaries in your personal and professional life to protect your emotional well-being. Learn to say no when necessary, delegate tasks, and create a healthy balance between work, relationships, and self-care. Setting boundaries promotes emotional regulation and prevents emotional burnout.

8. Engaging in self-care: Prioritize self-care as a regular practice to recharge and rejuvenate. This includes engaging in activities that bring you joy, nurturing your physical health through exercise and healthy habits, getting sufficient rest, and practicing self-compassion. Self-care supports emotional well-being and resilience.

By developing emotional regulation and stress management techniques, you enhance your ability to navigate and manage emotions effectively. Cultivate emotional awareness, practice mindfulness, explore stress reduction techniques, and develop healthy coping strategies. These practices empower you to regulate emotions, reduce stress, and foster emotional well-being and resilience in the face of life's challenges.

Cultivating self-compassion and practicing self-care

In this section, we will focus on cultivating self-compassion and practicing self-care as essential components of resilience and emotional well-being. Self-compassion involves treating yourself with kindness, understanding, and acceptance, while self-care encompasses nurturing your physical, mental, and emotional well-being.

1. Embracing self-compassion: Recognize the importance of self-compassion in building resilience and emotional well-being. Embrace self-compassion by offering yourself kindness and understanding, especially during challenging times. Treat yourself with the same care and compassion you would extend to a loved one.

2. Practicing self-acceptance: Cultivate self-acceptance by embracing your strengths, weaknesses, and imperfections. Recognize that nobody is perfect, and it is okay to make mistakes. Embrace your authentic self and let go of self-judgment and self-criticism.

3. Nurturing self-care routines: Establish self-care routines that prioritize your physical, mental, and emotional well-being. Engage in activities that replenish your energy and bring you joy and relaxation. This may include exercise, getting enough sleep, spending time in nature, engaging in hobbies, or practicing mindfulness and meditation.

4. Setting healthy boundaries: Learn to set healthy boundaries to protect your well-being and prevent emotional overwhelm. Clearly communicate your needs and limits to others, and prioritize time for yourself. Setting boundaries helps maintain a healthy balance between giving to others and nurturing

yourself.

5. Engaging in self-reflection: Dedicate time for self-reflection to gain deeper insights into your emotions, thoughts, and needs. Regularly check in with yourself, identify areas that require attention or support, and adjust your self-care practices accordingly. Self-reflection promotes self-awareness and guides your self-care journey.

6. Practicing self-compassionate self-talk: Pay attention to your inner dialogue and practice self-compassionate self-talk. Replace self-criticism and negative self-talk with kind and supportive words. Treat yourself as you would a close friend, offering encouragement, understanding, and validation.

7. Seeking support: Reach out for support when needed, whether it be from friends, family, or professionals. Recognize that seeking support is a sign of strength, not weakness. Share your challenges and emotions with trusted individuals who can provide a listening ear and valuable insights.

8. Prioritizing leisure and enjoyment: Make time for leisure and activities that bring you joy and pleasure. Engaging in hobbies, spending time with loved ones, or simply engaging in activities that bring you a sense of fulfillment contribute to your overall well-being and nourish your resilience.

By cultivating self-compassion and practicing self-care, you nurture your emotional well-being and build resilience. Embrace self-compassion as a guiding principle, establish self-care routines, set healthy boundaries, and engage in self-reflection. Prioritize your well-being and invest in activities and practices that replenish and rejuvenate your mind, body, and soul. Through self-compassion and self-care, you strengthen your resilience and create a solid foundation for emotional well-being.

Building meaningful connections and cultivating a support network

In this section, we will explore the importance of building meaningful connections and cultivating a support network as crucial elements of resilience and emotional well-being. Human connection and a sense of belonging contribute to our overall happiness and help us navigate life's challenges with greater resilience.

1. Nurture existing relationships: Invest time and effort in nurturing your existing relationships. Maintain open lines of communication, express appreciation and gratitude, and show genuine interest in the lives of others. Strong, meaningful connections provide emotional support and a sense of belonging.

2. Foster new connections: Seek opportunities to meet new people and expand your social circle. Engage in activities or join groups and communities that align with your interests and values. Building new connections broadens your support network and offers diverse perspectives and experiences.

3. Practice active listening: Practice active listening in your interactions with others. Give your full attention, maintain eye contact, and listen with genuine interest and empathy. Active listening enhances understanding, strengthens connections, and promotes a sense of being heard and understood.

4. Show empathy and compassion: Cultivate empathy and compassion in your interactions. Seek to understand others' perspectives, validate their emotions, and offer support and understanding. Empathetic and compassionate connections create a safe space for emotional expression and foster deeper relationships.

5. Be a supportive presence: Be a supportive presence in the lives of those around you. Offer a lending ear, provide encouragement, and be available to support others during challenging times. Show up for others and let them know they

can count on you.

6. Seek support when needed: Recognize that it's okay to seek support from others when you are facing difficulties. Reach out to your support network for emotional support, guidance, or practical help. Asking for support is a sign of strength and vulnerability.

7. Engage in collaborative activities: Engage in collaborative activities that foster teamwork and a sense of community. This could include volunteering, participating in group projects, or joining clubs or organizations that align with your interests. Collaborative activities strengthen connections and create a sense of belonging.

8. Practice forgiveness and understanding: Foster forgiveness and understanding in your relationships. Let go of grudges and resentments, and approach conflicts with a willingness to understand and find common ground. Cultivating forgiveness and understanding promotes harmonious relationships and emotional well-being.

By building meaningful connections and cultivating a support network, you strengthen your resilience and emotional well-being. Nurture existing relationships, foster new connections, practice active listening, and show empathy and compassion. Be a supportive presence in the lives of others and seek support when needed. Engaging in collaborative activities and practicing forgiveness and understanding enhance your connections and contribute to a more resilient and fulfilling life.

Chapter 5: Embracing Mindfulness and Finding Inner Balance

Understanding the principles of mindfulness and its impact on well-being

In this chapter, we will delve into the principles of mindfulness and explore how it can positively impact our well-being. Mindfulness is the practice of being fully present in the moment, cultivating non-judgmental awareness, and accepting our experiences without resistance. By embracing mindfulness, we can find inner balance, reduce stress, and enhance our overall well-being.

1. Definition of mindfulness: Gain a clear understanding of what mindfulness means. Mindfulness involves intentionally directing our attention to the present moment, observing our thoughts, emotions, and bodily sensations with curiosity and non-judgmental awareness. It is about being fully present and engaged in the here and now.
2. Cultivating non-judgmental awareness: Practice observing your thoughts, emotions, and sensations without judgment. Notice any tendency to label experiences as good or bad, and instead, adopt an attitude of curiosity and acceptance. By cultivating non-judgmental awareness, you can reduce self-criticism and cultivate self-compassion.
3. Living in the present moment: Shift your focus from dwelling on the past or worrying about the future to fully experiencing the present moment. Bring your attention to the sensations of your breath, the sounds around you, or the sensations in your body. By immersing yourself in the present, you can find peace and clarity.
4. Mindful breathing: Utilize the breath as an anchor to the

present moment. Take regular pauses throughout the day to focus on your breath, observing its rhythm and sensations. Deep, mindful breaths can help calm the mind, reduce stress, and promote a sense of relaxation.

5. Body scan meditation: Engage in body scan meditations to bring awareness to different parts of your body. Slowly scan from head to toe, noticing any sensations or tensions without judgment. This practice helps you develop a deeper connection with your body and cultivates a sense of relaxation and self-awareness.

6. Mindful eating: Bring mindfulness to your meals by savoring each bite, noticing the taste, texture, and aroma of the food. Slow down and eat without distractions, fully engaging your senses. Mindful eating fosters a healthier relationship with food, promotes gratitude, and enhances the enjoyment of the eating experience.

7. Accepting emotions and thoughts: Practice accepting your emotions and thoughts as they arise, without trying to suppress or control them. Allow them to come and go, observing them with gentle curiosity. By accepting them, you create space for self-reflection, emotional well-being, and a greater sense of inner balance.

8. Integrating mindfulness into daily life: Extend mindfulness beyond formal meditation practice and integrate it into your daily life. Bring mindful awareness to everyday activities such as walking, washing dishes, or interacting with others. By infusing mindfulness into your daily routines, you can cultivate a greater sense of presence and contentment.

By understanding the principles of mindfulness and incorporating its practices into your life, you can cultivate inner balance, reduce stress, and enhance your overall well-being. Embrace the present moment, cultivate non-judgmental awareness, and incorporate mindful practices into your daily life. The practice of mindfulness can bring about profound positive changes, promoting emotional, mental, and spiritual growth.

Practicing mindful self-care for holistic well-being

In this section, we will explore the concept of mindful self-care and its importance for achieving holistic well-being. Mindful self-care involves intentionally nurturing and tending to your physical, mental, and emotional needs with a sense of presence and self-compassion. By practicing mindful self-care, you can cultivate a deeper connection with yourself and enhance your overall well-being.

1. Self-compassion in self-care: Infuse self-compassion into your self-care practices. Treat yourself with kindness, understanding, and acceptance, especially during times of difficulty or when facing challenges. Approach self-care as an act of love and care for yourself.
2. Identifying your needs: Take time to identify your physical, mental, and emotional needs. Tune in to your body and emotions, and reflect on what you need to feel nourished and balanced. This could include rest, exercise, social connection, solitude, creative expression, or engaging in activities that bring you joy.
3. Engaging all senses: Incorporate mindfulness into self-care by engaging all your senses. Notice the sensations, smells, tastes, sounds, and visuals associated with your self-care practices. Fully immerse yourself in the present moment, savoring the experience with heightened awareness.
4. Creating a self-care routine: Establish a regular self-care routine that includes activities aligned with your needs and values. Set aside dedicated time for self-care and make it a non-negotiable part of your schedule. This consistent practice supports your

well-being and nurtures a sense of balance.

5. Mindful movement: Engage in mindful movement practices such as yoga, tai chi, or walking meditation. These practices combine physical movement with mindfulness, allowing you to connect with your body, release tension, and cultivate a sense of calm and well-being.

6. Setting boundaries: Practice setting healthy boundaries to protect your well-being. Learn to say no to activities or commitments that drain your energy or overwhelm you. Prioritize your needs and honor your limits to maintain a healthy balance in your life.

7. Unplugging from technology: Create moments of digital detox by consciously disconnecting from technology. Allocate dedicated time to unplug and engage in activities that nourish your well-being, such as reading, journaling, or spending time in nature. Disconnecting from technology allows for greater presence and rejuvenation.

8. Practicing gratitude: Cultivate gratitude as a part of your self-care routine. Take time each day to reflect on things you are grateful for, whether big or small. Gratitude cultivates a positive mindset, enhances overall well-being, and fosters a sense of contentment.

By practicing mindful self-care, you prioritize your holistic well-being and nurture a deeper connection with yourself. Embrace self-compassion, identify your needs, engage all your senses, and establish a self-care routine. Engage in mindful movement, set healthy boundaries, unplug from technology, and practice gratitude. Mindful self-care supports your overall well-being, enhances your relationship with yourself, and allows you to show up fully in your life.

Cultivating mindfulness in relationships for deeper connections

In this section, we will explore how to cultivate mindfulness in relationships to foster deeper connections, understanding, and empathy. Mindfulness can enhance the quality of your relationships by promoting presence, active listening, and compassion towards others. By incorporating mindfulness into your interactions, you can cultivate more meaningful and fulfilling connections with the people in your life.

1. Being fully present: Practice being fully present in your interactions with others. When engaging in conversations or spending time together, bring your attention to the present moment. Avoid distractions and give your undivided attention to the person you are with. Being present fosters deeper connections and shows respect and genuine interest.

2. Active listening: Cultivate the skill of active listening to demonstrate mindfulness in your relationships. Listen attentively without interrupting or preparing a response. Show genuine curiosity and empathy, seeking to understand the other person's perspective fully. Reflect back their words and feelings to convey your understanding.

3. Non-judgmental acceptance: Practice non-judgmental acceptance in your relationships. Avoid making assumptions or jumping to conclusions. Embrace an attitude of openness and acceptance, allowing others to express themselves freely without fear of judgment. Non-judgmental acceptance creates a safe space for honest communication and deepens trust.

4. Compassionate communication: Infuse compassionate communication into your interactions. Choose words and tones that convey empathy, kindness, and understanding. Speak from a place of mindfulness, considering the impact of your words on others. Practice patience and mindfulness even in challenging or conflictual situations.

5. Empathy and understanding: Cultivate empathy and

understanding towards others. Put yourself in their shoes, considering their thoughts, feelings, and experiences. Recognize that each person has their own unique perspective and validate their emotions. By practicing empathy, you foster deeper connections and create a supportive and caring environment.

6. Mindful conflict resolution: Apply mindfulness to conflict resolution by approaching disagreements with presence and compassion. Create a safe and non-threatening space for open dialogue. Practice active listening, validate each person's emotions, and seek collaborative solutions. Mindful conflict resolution enhances understanding and strengthens relationships.

7. Appreciation and gratitude: Cultivate a practice of appreciation and gratitude in your relationships. Regularly express appreciation for the presence and contributions of others in your life. Take time to acknowledge their qualities, efforts, and support. Expressing gratitude fosters positive emotions and deepens your connection with others.

8. Mindful acts of kindness: Engage in mindful acts of kindness towards others. Practice acts of generosity, compassion, and thoughtfulness without expecting anything in return. These acts can be simple gestures that demonstrate your care and appreciation for others. Mindful acts of kindness strengthen relationships and create a positive ripple effect.

By cultivating mindfulness in your relationships, you deepen connections, foster empathy, and create a more harmonious and fulfilling social environment. Practice being fully present, engage in active listening, practice non-judgmental acceptance, and communicate with compassion. Cultivate empathy, resolve conflicts mindfully, express appreciation, and engage in mindful acts of kindness. Mindfulness in relationships enriches your connections and promotes a more loving and supportive network of people in your life.

Applying mindfulness to stress management and emotional regulation

In this section, we will explore how to apply mindfulness to effectively manage stress and regulate emotions. Mindfulness can be a powerful tool in helping you navigate challenging situations with greater ease, resilience, and emotional balance. By incorporating mindfulness into your stress management and emotional regulation practices, you can cultivate a greater sense of calm and well-being.

1. Cultivating awareness of stress triggers: Develop an awareness of your personal stress triggers. Notice the thoughts, emotions, or situations that tend to evoke stress or overwhelm. By being mindful of your triggers, you can proactively respond to them in a more intentional and calm manner.

2. Mindful stress response: Practice a mindful stress response by taking a pause before reacting to stressful situations. Instead of immediately reacting with impulsive or habitual responses, take a few deep breaths and observe your thoughts and emotions with non-judgmental awareness. This allows you to respond consciously rather than reactively.

3. Body scan for stress release: Utilize the body scan technique to release tension and promote relaxation. Slowly scan your body from head to toe, noticing areas of tension or discomfort. As you observe these sensations, consciously release any tension or tightness, allowing yourself to relax and let go of stress.

4. Mindful breathing in stressful moments: When experiencing stress or overwhelm, bring your attention to your breath. Take slow, deep breaths, focusing on the sensation of the breath entering and leaving your body. This simple practice helps activate the body's relaxation response and calms the mind in

the midst of stress.

5. Labeling emotions: Develop the practice of labeling your emotions when you feel overwhelmed. As you experience strong emotions, name them without judgment, such as "anxiety," "frustration," or "sadness." Labeling emotions increases self-awareness and helps create distance between yourself and the emotions, allowing for a more mindful response.

6. Cultivating an observing mind: Foster the ability to observe your thoughts and emotions without getting entangled in them. Imagine yourself as an impartial observer, simply noticing the thoughts and emotions as they arise and pass. This practice cultivates a sense of detachment and reduces the intensity of emotional reactions.

7. Mindful self-compassion during stress: Practice self-compassion when faced with stress. Offer yourself words of kindness and understanding, acknowledging that stress is a natural part of life. Treat yourself with the same care and compassion you would extend to a friend, providing comfort and support during challenging times.

8. Mindfulness in daily stress management: Integrate mindfulness into your daily stress management practices. Take short mindfulness breaks throughout the day, engaging in mindful breathing, grounding exercises, or simply pausing to notice your surroundings. Regular mindfulness practice builds resilience and equips you to manage stress more effectively.

By applying mindfulness to stress management and emotional regulation, you can navigate challenging situations with greater ease and maintain emotional balance. Cultivate awareness of stress triggers, practice a mindful stress response, and utilize techniques such as body scans and mindful breathing. Label your emotions, foster an observing mind, and practice self-compassion during times of stress. Integrate mindfulness into your daily stress management practices to enhance resilience and promote overall well-being.

Chapter 6: Cultivating Positive Mindsets and Optimism

Understanding the power of positive mindsets and their impact on well-being

In this chapter, we will explore the power of positive mindsets and their profound impact on well-being. Positive mindsets involve cultivating optimistic perspectives, focusing on strengths, and embracing a positive outlook on life. By understanding and cultivating positive mindsets, you can enhance your overall well-being and resilience.

1. The role of positive thinking: Recognize the role of positive thinking in shaping your experiences and emotions. Positive thinking involves cultivating an optimistic and constructive outlook on life, focusing on possibilities, strengths, and opportunities. By adopting a positive mindset, you can approach challenges with resilience and embrace a more positive and fulfilling life.

2. Embracing a growth mindset: Cultivate a growth mindset, which believes that abilities and intelligence can be developed through effort and learning. Embrace challenges as opportunities for growth and view setbacks as stepping stones toward success. With a growth mindset, you foster a positive belief in your ability to learn, adapt, and overcome obstacles.

3. Cultivating gratitude: Practice gratitude as a way to cultivate a positive mindset. Regularly express gratitude for the blessings and positive aspects of your life. This practice shifts your focus towards appreciation, fostering positive emotions and a sense of abundance.

4. Reframing negative thoughts: Develop the skill of reframing negative thoughts into more positive and constructive ones.

Challenge negative self-talk and replace it with affirming and encouraging statements. Reframing helps shift your perspective and fosters a more positive and empowering mindset.

5. Practicing self-compassion: Cultivate self-compassion as a foundational element of positive mindsets. Treat yourself with kindness, understanding, and acceptance, especially during times of difficulty or when facing challenges. Practice self-compassion by offering yourself words of encouragement and support, embracing your imperfections, and acknowledging your efforts and progress.

6. Surrounding yourself with positivity: Create an environment that supports positive mindsets by surrounding yourself with positive influences. Seek out uplifting and inspiring content, surround yourself with supportive and optimistic individuals, and engage in activities that bring you joy and positivity.

7. Visualizing success and positive outcomes: Utilize visualization techniques to envision success and positive outcomes. Create mental images of your goals and aspirations, imagining yourself achieving them with confidence and joy. Visualizing success enhances motivation and reinforces a positive mindset.

8. Celebrating small victories: Acknowledge and celebrate your small victories along your journey. Recognize and appreciate your accomplishments, no matter how small they may seem. Celebrating these milestones reinforces a positive mindset and boosts self-confidence.

By understanding the power of positive mindsets and incorporating them into your life, you can enhance your overall well-being and resilience. Embrace positive thinking, cultivate a growth mindset, practice gratitude, reframe negative thoughts, and prioritize self-compassion. Surround yourself with positivity, visualize success, and celebrate your victories. Cultivating positive mindsets empowers you to approach life with optimism, resilience, and a greater sense of fulfillment.

Cultivating positive relationships and fostering a supportive network

In this section, we will explore the importance of cultivating positive relationships and fostering a supportive network for your well-being and personal growth. Positive relationships contribute to your overall happiness, provide emotional support, and offer opportunities for personal development. By actively nurturing positive relationships, you can enhance your well-being and build a strong support system.

1. Building authentic connections: Foster authentic connections with others by being genuine, open, and vulnerable. Engage in meaningful conversations and actively listen to others. Show genuine interest in their lives, thoughts, and experiences. Building authentic connections creates a sense of trust and mutual understanding.
2. Surrounding yourself with positive influences: Choose to surround yourself with positive influences that uplift and inspire you. Seek out relationships with individuals who share similar values, have a positive outlook on life, and encourage your personal growth. Positive influences provide support and motivation on your journey.
3. Nurturing supportive friendships: Invest time and effort into nurturing supportive friendships. Cultivate relationships with individuals who genuinely care about your well-being, provide emotional support, and celebrate your successes. Foster a give-and-take dynamic in which you support and uplift each other.
4. Cultivating kindness and empathy: Cultivate kindness and empathy in your interactions with others. Show compassion, understanding, and empathy towards their experiences and emotions. Small acts of kindness and empathy can create a

positive ripple effect, fostering deeper connections and mutual support.

5. Effective communication: Practice effective communication skills to foster positive relationships. Express your thoughts and feelings clearly and respectfully, and actively listen to others without judgment or interruption. Effective communication promotes understanding, trust, and mutual respect.

6. Resolving conflicts constructively: Approach conflicts in relationships with a constructive mindset. Seek resolution through open and honest communication, active listening, and a willingness to find common ground. Constructive conflict resolution strengthens relationships and deepens understanding.

7. Cultivating a support network: Build a support network of individuals who uplift and support you during challenging times. These individuals can be friends, family members, mentors, or support groups. Lean on your support network for emotional support, guidance, and encouragement when needed.

8. Practicing reciprocity: Foster reciprocity in your relationships by offering support, encouragement, and assistance to others. Be willing to reciprocate the care and support you receive from your network. Practicing reciprocity strengthens bonds and fosters a sense of belonging.

By actively cultivating positive relationships and fostering a supportive network, you enhance your well-being and personal growth. Build authentic connections, surround yourself with positive influences, nurture supportive friendships, and cultivate kindness and empathy. Practice effective communication and constructive conflict resolution. Cultivate a support network and embrace reciprocity in your relationships. Positive relationships provide a sense of belonging, support, and personal development, contributing to your overall happiness and well-being.

Practicing self-reflection for personal growth and self-awareness

In this section, we will explore the practice of self-reflection as a powerful tool for personal growth and self-awareness. Self-reflection involves taking intentional time to examine your thoughts, emotions, and experiences, and gaining deeper insights into yourself. By engaging in regular self-reflection, you can cultivate self-awareness, gain clarity, and make conscious choices aligned with your values and goals.

1. Carving out dedicated self-reflection time: Set aside dedicated time for self-reflection in your routine. Create a quiet and comfortable space where you can focus inward without distractions. This intentional time allows you to dive deeper into your thoughts, emotions, and experiences.
2. Journaling: Use journaling as a self-reflection tool. Write freely without judgment, exploring your thoughts, feelings, and reflections on various aspects of your life. Journaling helps clarify your thoughts, process emotions, and gain valuable insights into yourself.
3. Asking reflective questions: Pose reflective questions to yourself during self-reflection. Examples include "What are my values and priorities?", "What areas of my life do I want to improve?", or "What am I grateful for?". Thought-provoking questions guide your self-reflection and promote introspection.
4. Exploring strengths and areas for growth: Reflect on your strengths and areas for growth. Acknowledge and celebrate your strengths, as they contribute to your confidence and well-being. Identify areas where you would like to grow and develop, setting intentions for personal growth.

5. Examining beliefs and mindset: Engage in self-reflection to examine your beliefs, attitudes, and mindset. Notice any limiting beliefs or negative thought patterns that may be holding you back. Challenge and reframe these beliefs to cultivate a more empowering and growth-oriented mindset.

6. Assessing goals and progress: Reflect on your goals and assess your progress. Review your short-term and long-term goals, identify any adjustments or refinements needed, and celebrate milestones along the way. Regularly assessing your goals keeps you aligned with your aspirations.

7. Noticing patterns and triggers: Pay attention to patterns and triggers in your thoughts, emotions, and behaviors. Observe recurring themes or reactions that arise in certain situations. Self-reflection allows you to become more aware of these patterns and triggers, empowering you to respond consciously rather than reactively.

8. Cultivating self-compassion and acceptance: Practice self-compassion and acceptance during self-reflection. Embrace yourself with kindness, understanding, and acceptance, even when reflecting on areas for improvement. Self-compassion creates a safe space for growth and supports your overall well-being.

By engaging in regular self-reflection, you foster personal growth, deepen self-awareness, and make conscious choices aligned with your values and goals. Carve out dedicated self-reflection time, use journaling as a tool, and ask reflective questions. Explore your strengths and areas for growth, examine beliefs and mindset, and assess goals and progress. Notice patterns and triggers, and cultivate self-compassion and acceptance. Self-reflection is a powerful practice that nurtures your personal growth journey and enhances your self-awareness.

Harnessing the power of self-discipline and goal setting

In this section, we will explore the importance of self-discipline and goal setting in personal growth and achievement. Self-discipline is the ability to control your impulses, stay focused, and take consistent action towards your goals. By harnessing the power of self-discipline and setting clear goals, you can overcome obstacles, stay motivated, and make progress towards your aspirations.

1. Clarifying your goals: Take time to clarify your goals and aspirations. Reflect on what you want to achieve in different areas of your life, such as career, relationships, health, or personal development. Define specific, measurable, attainable, relevant, and time-bound (SMART) goals that align with your values and vision.

2. Breaking goals into actionable steps: Break down your goals into smaller, actionable steps. Identify the specific actions or milestones that need to be accomplished along the way. Breaking goals into manageable steps makes them more attainable and helps you maintain focus and momentum.

3. Creating a routine: Establish a routine that supports your goals and enables you to stay disciplined. Designate specific times and dedicate consistent effort towards working on your goals. Having a routine helps build discipline by making actions habitual and reducing the reliance on willpower alone.

4. Developing self-discipline habits: Cultivate self-discipline habits that support your progress. Identify key habits that align with your goals and commit to practicing them consistently. For example, if your goal is to improve your physical fitness, establish a habit of regular exercise or healthy eating.

5. Managing distractions and temptations: Learn to manage distractions and temptations that can derail your progress. Identify potential triggers or distractions that may interfere with your focus and develop strategies to overcome them. This

may include setting boundaries, creating an environment conducive to your goals, or practicing mindfulness to stay present.

6. Building resilience in the face of setbacks: Embrace setbacks as learning opportunities and build resilience in the face of challenges. Understand that setbacks are a natural part of the journey towards achieving your goals. Cultivate a growth mindset that sees obstacles as stepping stones to success, and persevere through setbacks with determination.

7. Seeking accountability and support: Seek accountability and support to help maintain discipline and stay on track. Share your goals with trusted individuals who can provide encouragement, guidance, and hold you accountable. Joining a supportive community or working with a mentor can also provide valuable accountability and motivation.

8. Celebrating milestones and progress: Celebrate your milestones and acknowledge your progress along the way. Recognize and reward yourself for the efforts and achievements, no matter how small. Celebrating milestones boosts motivation, reinforces positive habits, and provides a sense of accomplishment.

By harnessing the power of self-discipline and setting clear goals, you can make consistent progress towards your aspirations. Clarify your goals, break them into actionable steps, establish a routine, and develop self-discipline habits. Manage distractions and temptations, build resilience in the face of setbacks, seek accountability and support, and celebrate milestones and progress. Embracing self-discipline and goal setting empowers you to overcome obstacles, stay motivated, and achieve personal growth and success.

Chapter 7: Cultivating Resilience: Building Inner Strength in the Face of Challenges

Understanding resilience and its role in personal growth and well-being

In this chapter, we will explore the concept of resilience and its vital role in personal growth and well-being. Resilience refers to the ability to bounce back from adversity, adapt to change, and maintain a positive outlook despite challenges. By understanding resilience and cultivating it in your life, you can build inner strength, navigate difficult circumstances, and thrive in the face of adversity.

1. Definition of resilience: Gain a clear understanding of what resilience means. Resilience is the capacity to recover, adapt, and grow stronger from setbacks, adversity, or stress. It involves developing the psychological and emotional tools to cope with challenges and maintain a positive mindset.
2. Embracing a growth mindset: Cultivate a growth mindset as a foundation for resilience. Embrace the belief that challenges and setbacks are opportunities for growth and learning. With a growth mindset, you view obstacles as stepping stones to success and maintain a positive outlook even in difficult times.
3. Developing emotional intelligence: Foster emotional intelligence to enhance resilience. Emotional intelligence involves understanding and managing your own emotions and those of others. By developing emotional awareness, regulation, and empathy, you can navigate challenging situations with greater resilience and empathy.
4. Building a strong support system: Cultivate a strong support system of family, friends, mentors, or support groups. Surround yourself with individuals who provide encouragement,

understanding, and a sense of belonging. A strong support system offers emotional support, different perspectives, and practical assistance during challenging times.

5. Practicing self-care: Prioritize self-care as a means of building resilience. Engage in activities that promote physical, mental, and emotional well-being. Take care of your physical health through exercise, restful sleep, and a balanced diet. Nurture your mental and emotional well-being through relaxation, hobbies, and self-reflection practices.

6. Developing problem-solving skills: Enhance your problem-solving skills to navigate challenges effectively. Adopt a proactive and solution-oriented mindset when faced with obstacles. Break down problems into manageable steps, seek alternative perspectives, and explore different strategies to overcome challenges.

7. Cultivating optimism and positive thinking: Foster optimism and positive thinking as a way to bolster resilience. Maintain a positive outlook, focus on possibilities, and reframe setbacks as opportunities for growth. Embrace gratitude, practice positive affirmations, and seek out inspiring and uplifting content.

8. Practicing adaptability and flexibility: Develop adaptability and flexibility in your approach to challenges and change. Embrace uncertainty as a natural part of life and be open to adjusting your plans or perspectives when needed. Adapting to new situations with resilience allows you to navigate transitions more effectively.

By understanding resilience and incorporating it into your life, you can build inner strength and thrive in the face of challenges. Embrace a growth mindset, develop emotional intelligence, build a strong support system, and prioritize self-care. Enhance problem-solving skills, cultivate optimism and positive thinking, practice adaptability, and embrace change. Cultivating resilience empowers you to face adversity with strength, maintain a positive outlook, and continue growing on your personal journey.

Building resilience through self-reflection and learning from adversity

In this section, we will explore how self-reflection and learning from adversity can contribute to building resilience. Self-reflection allows you to gain insights, process emotions, and learn from challenging experiences. By embracing self-reflection and using adversity as a catalyst for growth, you can cultivate resilience and bounce back stronger from life's difficulties.

1. Embracing self-reflection: Embrace self-reflection as a tool for personal growth and building resilience. Set aside dedicated time to reflect on challenging experiences, examining your thoughts, emotions, and reactions. Self-reflection helps you gain perspective, understand patterns, and identify areas for growth.
2. Processing emotions: Allow yourself to process and express your emotions related to adversity. Validate your feelings without judgment or suppression. Engage in activities such as journaling, meditation, or talking to a trusted confidant to explore and release emotions in a healthy way.
3. Identifying lessons and growth opportunities: Seek lessons and growth opportunities within adversity. Reflect on what you have learned from challenging experiences and how they have contributed to your personal development. Identify strengths and skills that emerged or were strengthened as a result of overcoming adversity.
4. Cultivating a resilient mindset: Develop a resilient mindset by reframing adversity as a chance for growth and learning. Embrace the belief that you have the inner resources to

overcome challenges and bounce back stronger. View setbacks as temporary and setbacks rather than permanent failures.

5. Building problem-solving skills: Use adversity as an opportunity to develop and enhance problem-solving skills. Identify the specific challenges you faced and reflect on the strategies you employed to overcome them. Consider alternative approaches and explore new problem-solving techniques that can be applied in future situations.

6. Cultivating self-compassion: Practice self-compassion during self-reflection on adversity. Treat yourself with kindness, understanding, and acceptance, recognizing that facing challenges is a part of life. Offer yourself words of encouragement and support, acknowledging your efforts and resilience in navigating difficult circumstances.

7. Seeking support and learning from others: Engage in conversations with others who have faced similar challenges or have overcome adversity. Learn from their experiences, insights, and coping strategies. Seek support from mentors, support groups, or individuals who can provide guidance and encouragement during challenging times.

8. Cultivating adaptability and resilience through learning: Embrace a mindset of continuous learning and adaptation in the face of adversity. Be open to acquiring new skills, knowledge, and perspectives that can help you navigate future challenges. Approach each experience as an opportunity for personal growth and resilience-building.

By incorporating self-reflection and learning from adversity into your life, you can cultivate resilience and bounce back stronger from difficult experiences. Embrace self-reflection, process emotions, and identify lessons and growth opportunities. Cultivate a resilient mindset, build problem-solving skills, and practice self-compassion. Seek support and learn from others who have overcome adversity. Embrace adaptability and resilience through a commitment to lifelong learning. Building resilience through self-reflection and learning allows you to navigate future challenges with greater strength, wisdom, and confidence.

Cultivating resilience through self-care and stress management

In this section, we will explore how self-care and stress management practices contribute to cultivating resilience. Taking care of yourself and managing stress effectively can build your capacity to handle challenges, bounce back from adversity, and maintain overall well-being. By prioritizing self-care and implementing stress management strategies, you can enhance your resilience and thrive in the face of adversity.

1. Prioritizing self-care: Make self-care a priority in your life. Engage in activities that nourish your physical, mental, and emotional well-being. This may include regular exercise, adequate sleep, healthy eating, relaxation techniques, and engaging in hobbies or activities that bring you joy and fulfillment.
2. Developing healthy coping mechanisms: Cultivate healthy coping mechanisms to manage stress effectively. Identify strategies that help you relax, recharge, and regain emotional balance. This may involve deep breathing exercises, mindfulness or meditation practices, spending time in nature, or engaging in creative outlets.
3. Establishing boundaries: Set healthy boundaries to protect your well-being and manage stress. Learn to say no to excessive demands or commitments that may overwhelm you. Prioritize your needs and allocate time and energy for self-care activities. Setting boundaries helps you maintain balance and prevent burnout.
4. Seeking social support: Cultivate a strong support system of

trusted friends, family, or support groups. Seek social support when facing challenges or adversity. Connect with others who can provide emotional support, lend a listening ear, offer different perspectives, or provide practical assistance when needed.

5. Building resilience through positive relationships: Cultivate positive relationships that foster resilience. Surround yourself with individuals who uplift, inspire, and support you during challenging times. Engage in open and honest communication, share experiences, and seek guidance and encouragement when necessary.

6. Practicing stress management techniques: Implement stress management techniques to regulate your stress response. This may include deep breathing exercises, progressive muscle relaxation, engaging in physical activity, practicing mindfulness, or engaging in activities that promote relaxation and stress reduction.

7. Cultivating optimism and positive thinking: Foster optimism and positive thinking as tools for resilience. Focus on the possibilities and potential for growth, even in challenging situations. Embrace a positive mindset and reframe setbacks as opportunities for learning and personal development.

8. Seeking professional help when needed: Recognize when professional help may be beneficial in managing stress and building resilience. If stress becomes overwhelming or affects your overall well-being, consider seeking guidance from mental health professionals who can provide support, tools, and strategies for coping.

By incorporating self-care and stress management practices into your life, you can cultivate resilience and effectively navigate challenges. Prioritize self-care, develop healthy coping mechanisms, establish boundaries, and seek social support. Build resilience through positive relationships, practice stress management techniques, cultivate optimism and positive thinking, and consider seeking professional help when needed. Through these practices, you can enhance your ability to bounce back from adversity, maintain well-being, and thrive in the face of challenges.

Fostering resilience through a growth mindset and reframing challenges

In this section, we will explore how fostering a growth mindset and reframing challenges can contribute to building resilience. A growth mindset emphasizes the belief that abilities and intelligence can be developed through effort, learning, and embracing challenges. By cultivating a growth mindset and reframing challenges as opportunities for growth, you can enhance your resilience and thrive in the face of adversity.

1. Embracing a growth mindset: Adopt a growth mindset, which believes that skills, intelligence, and abilities can be developed through dedication and effort. Embrace challenges as opportunities for growth and learning, rather than viewing them as threats or obstacles. Cultivate a mindset that values effort, perseverance, and continuous improvement.

2. Reframing challenges as opportunities: Reframe challenges as opportunities for personal growth and resilience. Instead of seeing difficulties as roadblocks, view them as chances to learn, develop new skills, and strengthen your resilience. Shift your perspective to see challenges as stepping stones toward success and embrace the learning experiences they offer.

3. Cultivating a positive outlook: Cultivate a positive outlook in the face of challenges. Focus on the potential for growth, positive outcomes, and solutions, rather than dwelling on negative aspects or setbacks. Maintain an optimistic attitude and look for lessons and silver linings even in the most

challenging situations.

4. Developing problem-solving skills: Enhance your problem-solving skills to navigate challenges effectively. Embrace a proactive approach to problem-solving by breaking down challenges into smaller, manageable steps. Seek alternative perspectives, brainstorm creative solutions, and be open to adapting your strategies as needed.

5. Practicing self-compassion and self-encouragement: Practice self-compassion and self-encouragement during challenging times. Treat yourself with kindness, understanding, and patience, especially when facing setbacks or difficulties. Offer yourself words of encouragement and remind yourself of your resilience, strengths, and past successes.

6. Learning from failure: View failure as a valuable learning experience and an opportunity for growth. Embrace the lessons that failures can teach and use them as stepping stones toward future success. Emphasize the effort, progress, and lessons learned, rather than solely focusing on the outcome.

7. Seeking support and learning from others: Seek support from others who have overcome similar challenges or have cultivated resilience in their own lives. Learn from their experiences, insights, and strategies for building resilience. Surround yourself with individuals who inspire and support your growth mindset.

8. Engaging in continuous learning and personal development: Foster resilience by engaging in continuous learning and personal development. Stay curious, seek new knowledge, and pursue opportunities for growth and self-improvement. Embrace challenges as chances to expand your skills, knowledge, and capabilities.

By fostering a growth mindset and reframing challenges, you can enhance your resilience and thrive in the face of adversity. Embrace a growth mindset, reframe challenges as opportunities, and maintain a positive outlook. Develop problem-solving skills, practice self-compassion, and learn from failure. Seek support and learn from others, and engage in continuous learning and personal development. By adopting these approaches, you can cultivate resilience, adaptability, and a stronger belief in your ability to overcome challenges and achieve your goals.

Chapter 8: Embracing Change: Navigating Transitions and Embracing Personal Transformation

Understanding the nature of change and its role in personal growth

In this chapter, we will explore the nature of change and its significance in personal growth and transformation. Change is an inevitable part of life, and embracing it can lead to personal development, expanded perspectives, and new opportunities. By understanding the nature of change and its potential for growth, you can navigate transitions with resilience and embrace personal transformation.

1. Recognizing the constant presence of change: Understand that change is a natural and constant aspect of life. Everything around us, including ourselves, is in a state of continuous flux. By acknowledging and accepting the inevitability of change, you can approach it with greater openness and adaptability.

2. Embracing uncertainty: Embrace the inherent uncertainty that comes with change. Recognize that not all aspects of change can be controlled or predicted. Cultivate a mindset that sees uncertainty as an opportunity for growth, learning, and new experiences.

3. Viewing change as an opportunity for growth: Shift your perspective to see change as an opportunity for personal growth and transformation. Recognize that periods of transition and change often bring new possibilities, insights, and self-discovery. Embrace change as a chance to step out of your comfort zone and explore new horizons.

4. Building resilience in the face of change: Cultivate resilience to navigate and adapt to change effectively. Develop the ability to bounce back from setbacks, adjust to new circumstances, and

maintain a positive outlook during periods of change. Resilience enables you to face challenges with strength and flexibility.

5. Embracing a growth mindset: Adopt a growth mindset when faced with change. Embrace the belief that change provides an opportunity for learning, development, and personal evolution. See change as a chance to acquire new skills, expand your knowledge, and embrace new perspectives.

6. Letting go of attachments: Practice letting go of attachments to the past or the familiar when faced with change. Understand that clinging to old ways can hinder personal growth and hinder your ability to embrace new opportunities. By letting go of attachments, you create space for new experiences and possibilities.

7. Cultivating adaptability: Develop adaptability as a key trait for navigating change. Learn to adjust and adapt to new circumstances, environments, and demands. Embrace flexibility and openness, allowing yourself to flow with the changes rather than resisting them.

8. Seeking support during transitions: Reach out for support during times of change and transition. Lean on trusted friends, family members, mentors, or support groups who can provide guidance, encouragement, and perspective. Surround yourself with a supportive network that understands the challenges of change.

By understanding the nature of change and its potential for personal growth, you can navigate transitions with resilience and embrace personal transformation. Recognize the constant presence of change, embrace uncertainty, and view change as an opportunity for growth. Build resilience, adopt a growth mindset, and let go of attachments. Cultivate adaptability, seek support, and embrace the transformative power of change. Embracing change allows you to expand your horizons, discover new possibilities, and evolve into the best version of yourself.

Developing strategies for navigating change effectively

In this section, we will explore strategies for navigating change effectively and embracing personal transformation. Change can be challenging, but with the right mindset and approach, you can adapt, grow, and thrive amidst transitions. By developing effective strategies for navigating change, you can embrace the opportunities it presents and navigate through uncertainty with confidence.

1. Cultivating self-awareness: Develop self-awareness to understand your emotions, reactions, and triggers during periods of change. Pay attention to how you respond to change and identify any patterns or resistance that may arise. Self-awareness helps you navigate change with greater clarity and emotional intelligence.

2. Setting intentions and goals: Set intentions and goals to guide your journey through change. Clarify what you want to achieve or how you want to grow during the transition. Setting clear intentions and goals provides direction and motivation, helping you stay focused and committed throughout the process.

3. Embracing a positive mindset: Cultivate a positive mindset when navigating change. Embrace the belief that change brings opportunities for growth and new experiences. Practice gratitude, focus on the positives, and maintain an optimistic outlook, even during challenging times. A positive mindset fuels resilience and helps you navigate change with a proactive attitude.

4. Building a support network: Surround yourself with a supportive network of individuals who can offer guidance,

encouragement, and understanding during times of change. Seek out mentors, friends, or support groups that have experienced similar transitions. Sharing your journey with others provides valuable support and perspective.

5. Developing adaptability and flexibility: Cultivate adaptability and flexibility to navigate change effectively. Embrace the need to adjust your plans, perspectives, and approaches as circumstances evolve. Develop the ability to pivot, find alternative solutions, and embrace new opportunities that arise during the transition.

6. Practicing self-care: Prioritize self-care during periods of change to maintain your well-being and resilience. Engage in activities that nourish your mind, body, and spirit. Prioritize rest, relaxation, exercise, healthy eating, and activities that bring you joy and help you recharge.

7. Seeking learning and growth opportunities: Embrace change as an opportunity for learning and personal growth. Stay curious, seek new knowledge, and be open to acquiring new skills or perspectives. Look for ways to expand your comfort zone, step into new roles, or explore different areas of interest.

8. Reflecting and adapting along the way: Regularly reflect on your progress, lessons learned, and areas for adjustment during the change process. Be open to refining your strategies, adapting your goals, and making course corrections based on new insights and experiences. Reflecting and adapting help you stay aligned with your intentions and navigate change more effectively.

By developing strategies for navigating change effectively, you can embrace personal transformation and navigate transitions with greater ease. Cultivate self-awareness, set intentions and goals, embrace a positive mindset, and build a support network. Develop adaptability, practice self-care, seek learning opportunities, and reflect and adapt along the way. These strategies empower you to navigate change with resilience, purpose, and a sense of personal growth.

Cultivating resilience through self-reflection and learning from change

In this section, we will explore how self-reflection and learning from change can contribute to cultivating resilience. Self-reflection allows you to gain insights, process emotions, and extract valuable lessons from the experiences of change. By embracing self-reflection and actively learning from change, you can enhance your resilience and adaptability, fostering personal growth and transformation.

1. Engaging in self-reflection: Embrace self-reflection as a tool for understanding your thoughts, emotions, and reactions to change. Set aside dedicated time to reflect on the impact of change on your life, relationships, and personal growth. Self-reflection provides valuable insights and helps you navigate the complexities of change.
2. Processing emotions: Allow yourself to process and express your emotions related to the changes you're experiencing. Give space to feelings of uncertainty, fear, or excitement. Engage in activities such as journaling, meditation, or talking to a trusted confidant to explore and release emotions in a healthy way.
3. Identifying lessons and growth opportunities: Seek lessons and growth opportunities within the experience of change. Reflect on what you have learned about yourself, others, and the world around you through the process of change. Identify the strengths, skills, and resilience that have emerged or been strengthened as a result of navigating change.
4. Embracing the unknown: Embrace the unknown that accompanies change. Recognize that change often brings uncertainty and challenges, but it also opens doors to new

possibilities and personal growth. Embracing the unknown with a sense of curiosity and openness allows you to discover new paths and opportunities.

5. Adapting and adjusting: Practice adaptability and flexibility during times of change. Be willing to adjust your plans, perspectives, and expectations as circumstances evolve. Embrace the need to adapt and learn new skills or approaches that align with the changing landscape.

6. Cultivating a growth mindset: Foster a growth mindset when navigating change. Embrace the belief that challenges and setbacks are opportunities for learning and personal development. View change as a chance to acquire new knowledge, skills, and perspectives that contribute to your growth and resilience.

7. Celebrating progress and milestones: Celebrate your progress and milestones along the journey of change. Acknowledge and appreciate the steps you have taken, the challenges you have overcome, and the growth you have achieved. Celebrating milestones reinforces positive habits, boosts motivation, and reinforces resilience.

8. Seeking support and learning from others: Seek support from others who have navigated similar changes or have cultivated resilience in their own lives. Learn from their experiences, insights, and strategies for adapting to change. Surround yourself with a supportive network that understands the challenges and opportunities of change.

By embracing self-reflection and actively learning from change, you can cultivate resilience and adaptability. Engage in self-reflection, process emotions, and identify lessons and growth opportunities. Embrace the unknown, practice adaptability, and cultivate a growth mindset. Celebrate progress and seek support from others who have navigated change successfully. By actively learning from change, you can enhance your resilience and foster personal growth and transformation.

Nurturing self-compassion and practicing self-care during change

In this section, we will explore the importance of nurturing self-compassion and practicing self-care during times of change. Change can be challenging and demanding, making it crucial to prioritize your well-being and extend kindness and care towards yourself. By nurturing self-compassion and practicing self-care, you can enhance your resilience, maintain balance, and navigate change with greater ease.

1. Cultivating self-compassion: Cultivate self-compassion as a way to support yourself during times of change. Treat yourself with kindness, understanding, and acceptance. Recognize that change can be difficult and that you may face setbacks or challenges along the way. Offer yourself words of encouragement and remind yourself that you are doing the best you can.

2. Practicing self-care: Prioritize self-care as a means of maintaining your well-being during change. Engage in activities that nourish your mind, body, and spirit. Make time for restful sleep, regular exercise, nutritious meals, and activities that bring you joy and relaxation. Self-care replenishes your energy and resilience.

3. Setting boundaries: Establish clear boundaries to protect your well-being during times of change. Recognize your limits and prioritize self-care by saying no to excessive demands or commitments that may overwhelm you. Set aside dedicated time for self-reflection, self-care activities, and relaxation.

4. Seeking support: Reach out for support when needed. Surround yourself with a network of trusted friends, family, or mentors who can provide guidance, encouragement, and a

listening ear. Seek professional support if necessary, such as therapy or counseling, to navigate the emotional challenges that may arise during change.

5. Engaging in stress-reducing practices: Incorporate stress-reducing practices into your daily routine. This may include mindfulness meditation, deep breathing exercises, yoga, or engaging in activities that help you relax and unwind. These practices can help alleviate stress and promote emotional well-being.

6. Practicing self-reflection and self-awareness: Engage in self-reflection and self-awareness to understand your needs and emotions during times of change. Take time to check in with yourself and identify any areas of stress or overwhelm. Adjust your self-care practices as needed and listen to your intuition.

7. Maintaining healthy habits: Maintain healthy habits that support your well-being during change. Ensure you get enough sleep, eat balanced meals, and engage in regular physical activity. Prioritize activities that bring you joy, help you recharge, and foster a sense of stability amidst change.

8. Allowing for rest and rejuvenation: Give yourself permission to rest and rejuvenate during times of change. Pace yourself and avoid overexertion. Prioritize moments of relaxation, leisure, and self-reflection. Taking breaks allows you to replenish your energy and approach change with clarity and resilience.

By nurturing self-compassion and practicing self-care, you can enhance your resilience and well-being during times of change. Cultivate self-compassion, prioritize self-care activities, and set boundaries. Seek support when needed, engage in stress-reducing practices, and practice self-reflection and self-awareness. Maintain healthy habits and allow yourself time for rest and rejuvenation. Nurturing self-compassion and practicing self-care supports your resilience, balance, and ability to navigate change with grace and strength.

Embracing the transformative potential of change and fostering personal growth

In this section, we will explore how to embrace the transformative potential of change and foster personal growth. Change offers opportunities for self-discovery, learning, and transformation. By embracing change and actively seeking personal growth, you can navigate transitions with a sense of purpose and evolve into the best version of yourself.

1. Embracing a growth mindset: Adopt a growth mindset that embraces change as an opportunity for learning, growth, and personal development. Embrace the belief that your abilities and potential can be developed through effort, practice, and continuous learning. See change as a chance to expand your skills, knowledge, and perspectives.
2. Embracing discomfort and uncertainty: Be willing to step out of your comfort zone and embrace the discomfort and uncertainty that come with change. Growth often occurs outside of familiar territory. Challenge yourself to try new things, take calculated risks, and embrace the unknown.
3. Setting meaningful goals: Set meaningful goals that align with your values and aspirations. Use change as an opportunity to reassess your priorities and create goals that reflect your evolving needs and desires. Set clear, actionable, and inspiring goals that inspire you to stretch and grow.
4. Seeking new experiences and learning opportunities: Actively seek new experiences and learning opportunities during times of change. Engage in activities that challenge you, expose you to different perspectives, and broaden your horizons. Pursue

personal interests, enroll in courses, or participate in workshops to expand your knowledge and skills.

5. Reflecting on lessons learned: Take time to reflect on the lessons learned from your experiences of change. Consider the insights gained, the skills developed, and the personal growth that has occurred. Reflective practice allows you to integrate the lessons learned and apply them to future situations.

6. Cultivating resilience and adaptability: Foster resilience and adaptability as you navigate change. Build your capacity to bounce back from setbacks, remain flexible in the face of challenges, and adapt to new circumstances. Resilience and adaptability allow you to navigate change with strength and grace.

7. Seeking feedback and learning from others: Seek feedback from trusted individuals and learn from their perspectives. Embrace constructive feedback as an opportunity for growth and improvement. Engage in meaningful conversations with others who have experienced similar changes or have wisdom to share.

8. Embracing lifelong learning: Cultivate a commitment to lifelong learning and personal growth. See change as an ongoing opportunity to expand your knowledge, skills, and perspectives. Stay curious, pursue new interests, and embrace a mindset of continuous learning and development.

By embracing the transformative potential of change and fostering personal growth, you can navigate transitions with purpose and evolve into the best version of yourself. Embrace a growth mindset, step out of your comfort zone, and embrace discomfort and uncertainty. Set meaningful goals, seek new experiences, and reflect on lessons learned. Cultivate resilience and adaptability, seek feedback from others, and embrace lifelong learning. Embracing the transformative potential of change empowers you to navigate transitions with intention, embrace personal growth, and create a fulfilling and meaningful life.

In conclusion, "Mastering Emotional Intelligence: Enhancing Relationships and Self-Mastery" is a book that delves into the core principles of emotional intelligence, offering practical techniques to improve self-awareness, empathy, and communication skills. Throughout the chapters, we have explored various aspects of emotional intelligence, including self-reflection, self-regulation, social awareness, and relationship management. By incorporating the principles and strategies discussed in this book, readers can embark on a transformative journey towards mastering emotional intelligence, strengthening relationships, and achieving self-mastery.

Emotional intelligence is a crucial skill that allows us to understand and manage our emotions effectively. By developing self-awareness, we gain insight into our own emotional patterns, triggers, and strengths. This self-awareness forms the foundation for enhancing our emotional intelligence and becoming more attuned to the emotions of others.

Furthermore, self-regulation empowers us to manage our emotions and responses in a constructive manner. It involves developing techniques to manage stress, regulate emotional reactions, and make thoughtful decisions. By practicing self-regulation, we can navigate challenging situations with composure and adaptability.

Social awareness involves recognizing and understanding the emotions and needs of others. By cultivating empathy and active listening skills, we can deepen our connections, foster meaningful relationships, and enhance our ability to collaborate effectively.

Finally, relationship management focuses on applying emotional intelligence skills to build and maintain healthy relationships. This involves effective communication, conflict resolution, and the ability to inspire and influence others positively. By mastering relationship management, we can cultivate strong connections, resolve conflicts, and create harmonious environments.

Throughout this book, we have emphasized the importance of practice, self-reflection, and continuous learning. Emotional intelligence is a lifelong journey, and it requires dedication and commitment. By integrating the principles and strategies discussed in this book into our daily lives, we can enhance our emotional intelligence, strengthen our relationships, and achieve self-mastery.

In the pursuit of mastering emotional intelligence, it is essential to remember that it is a personal and individual journey. Each person's experience will be unique, and progress may come in different forms and at different times. The key is to approach this journey with openness, curiosity, and a willingness to grow and evolve.

"Mastering Emotional Intelligence: Enhancing Relationships and Self-Mastery" is a guide that encourages readers to embark on a transformative journey of self-discovery and emotional growth. By incorporating the principles and practices discussed in this book, readers can develop their emotional intelligence, improve relationships, and achieve self-mastery. May this book serve as a valuable resource and companion in your quest for emotional intelligence and personal transformation.

Don't miss out!

Visit the website below and you can sign up to receive emails whenever Christoffer Smestad publishes a new book. There's no charge and no obligation.

https://books2read.com/r/B-A-DDRW-BKTLC

BOOKS 2 READ

Connecting independent readers to independent writers.

Also by Christoffer Smestad

The Peloponnesian War Chronicles
The Peloponnesian War Chronicles: Power, Politics, and Conflict in Ancient Greece

Standalone
Mind Matters: A Guide to Emotional Wellness
The Power of Manifestation: How to Bring Your Dreams to Life
Addressing Climate Change and Human Health
AI in Action: A Comprehensive Guide to Real-world Applications
The Ukraine-Russia Conflict
Resilience Unleashed: The Persian Wars' Impact
Warbound: Epic Tales of Troy
Resilient Pages The Hidden Library
Unlock Your Potential
20 Life Skills You Don't Get Taught in School: A Practical Guide to Personal Growth and Success
Mastering Emotional Intelligence: Enhancing Relationships and Self-Mastery
the art of self-reflection: Nurturing Inner Growth through Introspection